Heinz Bartsch

The Positive German God-Belief

Letters to the German People of the
Twentieth Century after the Turning Point

New Edition for the Twenty-First Century, and with the
God-believers' Catechism, Published by
Imprimerie Ville de Papier, Cincinnati, O.
2022

Originally published in Germany, 1939, by Richard Queißer Verlag, Jauer in Schlesien.
Printing: Richard Quießer printing house, formerly Jauer's Tageblatt printing company Jauer i. Schlef.

Note on United States English Translation:
Under US law, the person who creates the translation secures copyright to the translated work, assuming that either (1) *an existing translation does not already have copyright*, or (2) the new translation is substantially different from an existing translation under copyright. The original work has since lapsed in its copyright, however all rights are reserved for this translation.

Translated to English by Siria and K. Lefebvre
Edited and Typeset by K. Lefebvre
February - July 2022
2022 © Imprimerie Ville de Papier
Cincinnati, O.
Printed in the United States of America
First Published Edition – October 2022
ISBN 978-1-7370610-4-5

It is Imperative
Not to End the Commandment of Life
Forever in vain!
That's why you must arise man!
and change your mind
sacrifice yourself to the commandments
in Freedom.

TABLE OF CONTENTS

The Positive German God-Belief

Foreword..8

About God, Faith, Life...11

From Destiny...39

From Guilt...44

The Commitment of the Will................................47

From the Eternal...49

The God-Believers' Catechism

Catechism..55

A Note from the Editor...61

FOREWORD

Everywhere in the German state presently and around the world people are asking about the "positive" German belief in God. Because this belief in God no longer denies or overlooks itself.

In questioning its existence, the Christian side seeks to deny it as atheism – or instill doubt among those who are ready and open to the German belief in God.

This document intends to serve both the divorce of that foreign belief and its supporters, and the ultimate decision to believe in one's own path.

A magical poison has been pouring into the European races for twenty centuries, for ten centuries they have given their faith to foreign administration. Now they are used to their dosage, or they finally awaken from this paralysis because they remain healthy enough to, and they will awaken the entire world.

Reflection and rejection, clarification and explanation, are necessary.

"Recognize yourself in your faith!" and decide according to it that it is not only a requirement of time, but a necessity of eternity, if truth, and thus human civilization is to be acknowledged.

—What can you recognize of yourselves in this faith?

I want to tell you. To see if it is not what you have always carried in you, clearly or indistinctly, consciously or unconsciously, and reaffirm that it is that which has made you relentless beings despite your Christianization.

Realize— in the end, people have to go out with only themselves. But whoever is a stranger in his own faith, who does not have complete communion with himself, cannot ultimately have it with his people.

Man is not without a people.

But without their foundation in faith, in existence, a people is nothing.

About God, Faith, Life.

The "positive" in "Positive God Belief" is God. God alone. Whoever denies it, denies God. Those who don't see it, are blind to God's existence.

The positive of life is a belief. A belief in God alone. From which everything comes. If you don't find it, you've never truly lived.

If everything is done right, faith will serve God in life. The fact that in Christianity, God and life serve faith, in the churches, makes this faith godless and lifeless.

The positive aspect of a belief is God! What is the positive aspect of God?

That you can't get past him. That you can't get past it itself. That without him, nothing can begin nor end. So be it.

How should we understand this?

Life is a reality that constantly imposes itself on everyone: through their experience.

And we experience so much, basically everything goes beyond our human capacity and comprehension. We become human, but because such experience is superhuman, it is broader than ourselves. And yet this also extends into us, is within us, is an entire experience, but never becomes complete knowledge.

And this infinite, superhuman aspect in every experience says: God! And at the same time lets us become aware of ourselves, in that our knowledge is always finite.

Because only in the mind, in knowledge, do we have fixed limits, approximate limits in each case; in this we acquire self-consciousness.

In contrast, in experiencing we embrace the whole world, we live through it, and yet grasp it nowhere. In experience we know nothing of the infinite, the unlimited, it overwhelms us because it is incomprehensible to us; we can't help it, we have to let it take hold of us, yet we cannot hold it. We may only find peace if we have obeyed him and heard this call: God! So only in the searching act, which is a restlessness of its own, and never eternal, can we find peace.

The infinite says: God! Yet this is not God. God is incomprehensible.

What cannot be understood is incomprehensible reality. In its experience, in the experience of all things, in which it rises and holds the center, we are gripped as if by a power which comes out of it and which we call God, in order to make this palatable to us.

So we know about God through an event, as well as an event horizon. Through an event within us that we have to concede, which we call God.

We know about God through the thirst for experience within us, to be receptive to the infinite, with our whole being. That the infinite may marry with the finite within us. From one time to another. Because there is no such thing as an eternal marriage with this existence. One thing must dissolve in the other, as in death.

Only eternal direction is truth.

The urge is the infinite within us, while the power and the drive are the finite within us. The urge comes from the infinite, while the strength strives in it.

The incomprehensible says: God! That means: We realize what our direction is through God, but not the direction of God.

We know of God. But nothing from God. Only from ourselves through him. Through God's reality, the incomprehensible work of our experience, which gives us direction and makes us conscious.

When we speak of God and "everything" (pantheism) or, "nothing" (materialism), "certainty" within us (mysticism) or outside of us (theism), "absolute" within and outside of us (the power in naturalism; the spirit in idealism), we desperately try to make him tangible, to make him human.

God grows in the world — God lives in its nature — God shapes life. Let us leave God incomprehensible. The more incomprehensible he is to us, the more powerfully he grasps us.

God is irrefutable within us. Through our experience.
God is demonstrable through us. Through our lives.
Faith is dedication to the world, it is a life conscious in God.
Faith is experiencing in God and life from God.

Therefore, we only ask about a creator when inside of us the urge and energy of the creation are in the body and soul, the mass's function is to take care of and protect.

Because everything else can questioned, it will be questioned.

The divine experience is the only thing outside of true inquiry. If we want and believe it ourselves.

Divine experience? Is God an experience?

God is not an experience. God is in the experience. In everyone's experience. Through our energy of experience, which causes it. Undefined "what" (to be) and "how" (to become), defining (to be) in men (to become). God "is" in our drive, and we "become" in our strength, want, attain, sufficiency for this drive.

We have God in our experience and experience everything in God. We experience beautiful, ugly, cheerful, and dark things in God. And only experience in God what is so beautiful, ugly, cheerful and dark. The soul seized by God is at the same time a soul that seizes God.

Without the people, God is not God.

We do not understand our last incomprehension and are ready for God in this incomprehension.

Just as the power of generation belongs to man without he having or could not have created himself, so the experience of God belongs to man without man having or could have done it.

In our experience God is like life in the body. Not adhering to any part, to be found with no knife, no microscope - and yet there!

Nothing itself without being nothing itself.

Incomprehensible!

We never get beyond that.

We experience ourselves in God. And live in God in our faith.

What is a belief then? What is a religion?

Something that comes from God and is aimed at God. The way that happens is the difference between belief or religion — and this depends as well on the type and race of a society.

How does faith or religion come from God in Christianity?

By the grace of God in Jesus Christ. By appearing visible in a man's body and through miracles (healings, predictions, resurrection), God proves his divinity as a supernatural being.

How does faith or religion lead to God in Christianity?

Through the grace of God in Jesus Christ. By men who try to prove to God of their right faith and life, consequent the succession of Christ.

In humility of everything, since it is God's plan, man no longer submits to the laws of life, because life in itself appears bad and corrupt.

Only the unnatural is close to God. So Christianity has its ideals in the charity of the lost, in monasticism, and in Internationalism.

Naturally, man knows nothing about God. God favors the repentant sinner more than the righteous. The most sinful person is the closest to God, because, mindful of his sins, he is the one who has repented the most, ergo the one who also believes the most in this tenet of the faith. And who would not want to be the most devout?

How did this idea of the repentant sinner, dearer to God than the righteous, spoil the soul of our people? Let his will weaken for salvation, and his willingness to deal with calamity, the unholy— proliferate. Our people were almost corrupted because of this Christian ideal of salvation.

The nature of this God makes his appearance most glorified in the most shamelessly decayed and unnatural people, irreverent in the consequences of their actions through penance, rather than seeking a path of righteous conviction. Hence salvation comes from the Jews.

The unique appearance of this God and the permanent connection to him, invisible and distant from human beings, requires a unique, eternal institution, which God represents in the visible and human, and into which man enters: the priestly church.

Church produces a connection to God based upon certain obligations. This connection (religion), its handling and achievement, that is Christianity. It is religion, not faith!

How does faith or religion become God in German culture?

Through the vitality of God in the human experience.

How does faith or religion lead to God in German culture?

Through the life of God in the events of man.

By a living God. Lived in nature. Experienced from the inner laws of inheritance, manifest in the outer laws of nature. So that our inheritance is naturally preserved in the creation of a culture, that is, of free human creation, and not removed from life.

In Germany, our culture is experienced from God and lived toward God. That means life that nourishes its light from the darkness and is therefore real life.

In the German culture, the nature of being is experienced obligatorily, a lived duty.

It is not the gap between life and experience, nature and God, that makes faith, but rather the duality of life and experience. Our last incomprehension is in God and fills our belief. Because solidarity with God is faith. Not religion. Religion is a faltering connection with God through an intermediary.

Life can also be without experiencing, and may keep itself in order even without such reflection, as proven by non-human nature. But experiencing cannot be without God and faith, otherwise life becomes disordered.

Unknowing nature, inevitably chooses the right things in the instinct of the animal and the plant. Knowing nature, that in man, arrives at situations with knowledge which may have unfounded conclusions and can therefore forget instinct. This happens when knowledge grows too burdensome. When knowledge becomes far from the immediate moment of life. When knowledge becomes hostile to it.

At times, people "forget", as our deep-seated German language so beautifully says, they can "forget" one's self. Man often does something to "forget", that is, to regain instinctive connection with life. Because the real life is almost never threatened by being in the present.

With knowledge there is always forgetting. If we were once without knowledge, then we "knew" everything like nature outside of us.

Now we are trying to recognize it. Recognize it again. Because all knowing is recognizing. The language already says so.

And therefore all that we recognize draws from the soul, which knows everything in its incomprehensibility.

The spirit penetrates this existence; but never its own causality because, it is its own condition.

The spirit only sees what is produced by the soul. It only sees that something comes out of it, it can not see all within. It throws a kind of light over the soul and waits whether something comes out of the soul at the right angle and straight, without shadows and blurred lines. This thing then becomes an understanding or realization! One calls it his realization.

Soul is needed in the world. Spiritual coercion of the world. To arrange oneself in a fixed area that the soul is taken for the most pressing need.

Spirit, will in the soul.
Will, soul in the spiritual.
And yet the darkness is eternal! And yet misery and want is eternal!

Because without darkness, God does not arise for man. And without struggle, man does not grow close to God.

Human struggle is the starting point of every belief, and religion. Man does not find his way in the infinite, he must let himself be directed outward of himself. Only then does his need and struggle become an external one.

Struggle is the starting point of every striving toward God. Religion, however, leaves man smaller than his need and calls on God repeatedly, only at his gracious help.

But faith shows God in the soul, and makes men greater than their need; which is misery and its struggle. Acting on this faith makes man an overcomer rather than a supplicant, a turner of his need, in triumph. Religion devaluates, faith reevaluates.
 Faith strengthens life, makes it right, strong, clear, meaningful, enriches it. Through constant struggle.

Religion finds it wrong, weak, unclear, senseless in itself even after every human effort, derides it with the promise of a better life thereafter, that is neither this life nor better.

In the German belief in God, one also strives to overcome life in the ordinary sense. But to enhance it. Not to destroy it.

Also in the German belief in God the slavish attachment to material goods is not meaningful, it does not imply divine right. But discipline in their use and increase for people, families, clans is a priority.

The spirit is not God even in such a belief. But also God is not spirit.

The spirit is also often an adversary to German belief in God. In some cases the spirit moves far away from life and finally denies itself, as in the Christian philosophy of idealism and materialism. Or in atheism, when one takes the place of the incomprehensible, in his self-confidence, and considers everything recognizable and knowable, as in modernity.

But the spirit is not the sun that keeps the dark earth alive. He is the moon which reflects it, that illuminates the night.

Life needs sun, it needs the soul that can make things grow. And needs the enlightened calm of the night that the spirit gives.

So the soul always grows: a natural faith proper of the countryside, belief that has its life-dependent fullness carved out of the need of its surroundings. Which is real, true, and beautiful in this landscape. Only in this landscape of the soul. In this faith, man finds life and experience as if placed between two rock faces.

As he sends his call out into life, so it comes back from experience as an echo. No matter how he turns and changes, he always has life in front of him and the echo of experience within him. His task manifests before him in life. In his experience he subconsciously arrives at his calling.

He never receives this power of experienced judgement explicitly. And yet it is there and never disappears in the back of his mind, lying dormant in intuition.

A man may want to shut off this small voice, but they can't. He would have to himself perish if he wanted to turn it off. And such instinct, as some call it, protects him from this. So long as the blood flows through his veins.

Who lives, cannot become godless.

What does the echo say about the nature of God?

Nothing! Only that it is God! That we end up somewhere in our energy and strength, where a power begins, that we can't suppress with all of our feelings. Which is the voice of all life.

What does the echo say about man?

Everything! As his echo exists, so man is alive, so his life coincides with the experience in God.

When faith and life let themselves lay into one another as if they were struggling, then the man fulfills a stronger, purer echo and carries it. Then a piece of life is fulfilled in him. Then the man is not helpless and without advice anymore in his movements, both the inner and outer ones. He stands, has his fixed place in the world, is carried by the echo and has at the same time his fixed direction, which, because of this, goes from fulfilment to fulfilment. Because he is fulfilled and brings this fulfilment with him. Do not search anywhere else. Outside. In things. In men.

He is always looking for pure and stronger echo in his life. Always struggling with the external and his inner nature. Because only in the struggle is there a clink, a tone, that resounds.

What is required, eternal, designed as an eternal echo within a person: that is his faith!

A people, and everything within it, grows in this echo. All living things are balanced in this echo, all living things try to condense into this reverberation.

Only if all individuals stand in the right and same way to life, are called into life in the same rhythm, will a single, strong and pure echo fill a valley of plenty, the spiritual space of a people. The life of a people will be fulfilled and sustained by the Eternal. A determined spiritual space is required in a way, in a race through life, binding this calling together. So is God alive.

Because God is the same primordial power everywhere, at all times and in all peoples. Only faith or religion, make everywhere, in all times and in all peoples, something different from the impulse and energy through God. This can only be done by a human being: the relief image of his kind.

According to the way in which life can be forced in a terrestrial space, has a kind, a race, arisen. According to this way, that's necessary to life, convictions and certainties that are such necessities become accustomed to the echo of the soul. These convictions and certainties are the basic laws of the species, that is, of faith.

They are insights that result from intentions. And vice versa. Faith is awareness of the species in knowing and wanting.

The nature of being is the appearance of a person's inner world in his belief. Faith, not some certification of external and internal physical characteristics, makes the race.

If a people has a belief, then it also has a closed nature, a determined way of being. If a person has part in this belief, he can participate, then he belongs to this type, this species.

So what can you see?

Not god! But certainly a belief in God!

One should not recognize God in his faith or even want to have recognized him; on the contrary, want to recognize and should have recognized his faith coming from God. This separates Christianity and Germanic faith to the fullest. In Christianity there is faith in God, the faith of the answered man in the long-revealed God. So is religion. And in German culture, there is faith from God, coming from the real, effective experience in God. Simply faith.

Must faith be recognized?

The infinite does not say: God! Immediately towards life?

So it said: God! And so it will be said again: God!

But to this day an idol, a stranger, still stands among us and will render it so we must break the base of it in order to be able to reach our earthly faith faith in freedom and perfection. For this task the the will of movement is required.

Our faith also lived under this cold, marble base. In the depths of the earth. There it must now be freed and, as a whole, visibly grow upward, into the light, as life grows from a dormant seed. What is required is the survival of the soul, the innermost turbulence of the heart, from which everyone sets themselves free and allows their spirit to be fully let out.

This faith has been formed in the depths like a crystal, which was prevented by an oppressive force from the full, free development of its essence, but in its dormant potential is nevertheless pure, designed for the complete form, always ready to become it. Tarnished and unclear externally due to the additions of depth and deposits of the heavy oppressive base. First, it needs a pillar of support. The knowledge of its peers giving growth above it. And the confession of its peers fed into it. That it was may finally stretch out and form in completion.

To put it in another picture, why is knowledge of the faith important, even with the soul's pressing influencing and the church finally removed from us: in order to be able to walk easily, we never needed the word for what we now call the "leg". However, in order to be able to walk again after a long period of infirmity, not only must the leg in the body as a whole be recognized, but also its innermost image and the function and laws of nature that affect it itself. So that this bodily organ may made healthy from our knowledge of its order, and must remain healthy.

We have many words, but we all lost the self-evident truth of our faith because of Christianity. We are sick in our faith. Or still weak as convalescents.

Every German person regards himself as sick in this alien faith. The entire German people and all Nordic peoples must recognize the picture and law of our kind and of our own beliefs. And what the movements of the present aim for indirectly concerns the political life, and directly the spiritual.

It is necessary to fully recognize the image and laws of our faith, in order to rediscover in ourselves what it is that was lost in consciousness. That the old Nordic man can arise anew.

Rise again. The new German man doesn't illustrate his experience of in the divine with any longer with the gods and goddesses once embodied by humanity, he does not seek to resurrect any more gods in myth, but lives according to the natural law of life. That primordial naivety of faith has been lost; it has cost him too many bitter experiences. Maybe Christianity was useful after all. Or we made it necessary.

The new German man has experienced too much impotence and powerlessness in his people to let the power of his faith out of his soul in pictures, to naively indulge in a world painting. He is still prepared now to constantly strike and counter-strike in the world. He sleeps with a girdled sword. His soul is as orderly as an encampment.

That is also why knowledge of the faith is necessary: so that one can look at himself in his totality and then knows how to keep ordered all the weakness, confusion and despair, that Christianity generates in abundance.

Through faith, man comes to himself in God.

By learning how to trust himself again, he lets his feeling raise objectively, sensing a pure echo.

By looking for God again, where does he find himself: in his own soul.

By worshiping God again, where does he honor himself: in his own life.

So faith is possible! Today and among the Germans! By being simple life experience and life decision in the experience of God.

Faith is possible because it is eternal growth of the soul, that cannot be manufactured and shaped, but can only be made conscious and put toward endless shaping.

Why is faith necessary?

So that life is lived responsibly, in duty. That God is through us in the faith of the inner law of the world, which must fit in with the reality of the outer. Our world of visions, our visions of the world.

The external world is examined through science. Yet science, in ignorance of its practice, is often mistaken for faith.

The reconciliation between science and faith is a matter of philosophy. It must not stand for faith, nor should it be confused with faith.

Philosophy has its own problem, as long as the world appears problematic in its divinity. It still too often today serves as an Aryan auxiliary science of a Jewish religion. Real philosophy can only be epistemology, a theory of knowledge that serves a life philosophy, that in turn is itself axiomatic, borne by faith.

Because fundamental ideas are not incompatible with the German belief in God. Rather, the German belief in God bears all living ideas in the German space. This belief is first and last through God.

Faith is necessary so that the species and its living forms can live in society responsibly. Neither the church nor state can assume complete responsibility for the convictions of a people.

Because if a decision should approach us as a whole, in our destiny as a people, which was not already grasped within ourselves, and which did not want to have its point of passage shape the world in our hands - without our duty, we have excluded ourselves from the vital existence of our species.

Have we become machines that require external energy? Are we no longer a living member who takes care of himself? That even the most vital community must finally wither.

Nobody can look into and reach into the soul. When there is no responsibility for one's own kind, it is worthless, indeed a danger for the living society.

The vitality and strength of the people is the measure of our life, our values. But not our experience. That lies solely in the divine echo of the soul of our people.

Faith is urge and strength.

Politics, the will and path.

Worldview, far-sightedness, the plan and order.

That is the triumph of German belief in God in a German worldview and politics. To settle a worldview means to discover its roots in the creating faith and to set free that faith. Those who have not reflected, felt through every detail, consciously or unconsciously, of their worldview, to the root of their beliefs, have neither this belief nor a coherent worldview firmly rooted in themselves.

Faith, that is the urge and the strength, through which the species appears in its own personal characteristics, is fulfilled in itself and remains alive in this fulfillment.

What about the security of one's belief?

In the German language, we do not say: I believe that. . . ., and don't we mean with that something uncertain?

Even if we use these words lightly or consciously, we let uncertainty resonate, thus uncertainty always lies in a purely bloody conviction, that has not yet developed in the reality that always wants to be realized.

So this is a fruitful, creative, thirsting insecurity that is inherent in a real belief. One which does not allow itself to be satisfied and satiated, which keeps existence alive in a tragic-heroic sense. This uncertainty pushes towards missionary work for the non-believers, who do not know if they can find another way in which they should get this belief. An uncertainty that doesn't leave room for dogma.

Is faith without limits?

Yes, faith is without limits, is limitless. Because that's the only way one has faith.

Is belief indefinable?

No! Faith is determinable, but not provable. Faith is conviction, not security. Conviction from what we want to ensure our lives: from our conscience. What we are certain of are the great insights and intentions of our species, from which we deny our life, only validly deny. Certainties from God have to be revived and developed, and images of God must not be created.

Experiencing God without conscience is mysticism.

Atmosphere, not determination. It prevailed when godly experience and conscience were not allowed to work together.

There is no conscience without God in the experience.

Where a person says conscience, God also says it through him.

Wherever a man is, there is also the uncertainty of life, security is urgently sought and finally only found out of certain insights and intentions that conscience reveals and has already set in, which one holds together in one's belief.

A soulfully, physically and mentally healthy person is also by nature a believer, a believer in God.

Faith is, with the necessity of race and species, experienced in the certainty of the living soul in the present conscience.

Neither scientific truth (objectivity) nor philosophical probability (speculation) nor historical certainty (concreteness) can and stand for this. Science must apply to all peoples, philosophy is always left to one's own interest, and history is always outdated.

Living conscience alone is connected to the species, and yet binding.

Even in one's wrong decisions. Because then the species is on the wrong path in reality, and will be corrected by the urge of the complete insecurity of life.

The individual evidence of conscience is not necessarily correct. Then there wouldn't be people, we would be completely on our own. There would be no struggle, no insecurity. But it is the life-saving, life-sustaining and life-strengthening statements that life itself proves.

Indeed, the security of faith can be found only in fact, it becomes the contrast of the certainty experienced in the conscience consecrated to God and the necessity of national existence, which is so experienced through historical fate. Certainty and necessity are not at all the same.

Where conscience fails on the personal or national side, it can only be straightened by reality itself. When a soul is no longer capable of experiencing and can no longer be guided to necessity through itself, no power of the external world is able to do so.

And as it is in the national existence, it is not so different in the personal. Finally a sense of real necessity is earned through the painful thrusts and emptiness of life and a full, satisfied life is lived— otherwise, when this sense is not earned, people remain in between resistance and self-denial.

Doubt is not a sign of godlessness, it is a sign of faith, which weighs experiences in the echo of the soul and makes decisions.

Namely faith from blood: faith from soul.

Faith from God.

God gives inner development through the urge. So the soul has the inner development in the power.

Blood and soul do not remain the same by nature; they develop the tangle of inheritance, the knot of hereditary factors, which according to the laws of life bind and release themselves. A new form in every person. Man is by nature not, a law, strict and exact. Were this the case, he wouldn't have a soul. He is never perfect, though he strives for ideals.

In the soul, which would be empty without blood, as blood is silent without the soul, properties degenerate and blossom. Because of external compulsion and the internal urge, which have formed the soul in the echo, and which will always form them, want to give energy a final form of reality.

Such development begins in the soul, activates a supporting spirit and ends again in the soul, as is the case with all development.

So knowledge is not decisive for faith and life, namely for a belief in life, but conscience is decisive alone!

No priest or book can tell one what they have experienced or cannot experience from one's soul. And once he has found this experience, a man has no need for some priest or book to speak for him!

If we wanted to save our German belief in God again in a book, in a "German Bible", which draws on the testimonies of our great past, this would mean a new interpretation and teaching, dogma and learning, and from that we would shrink a lot more on our own.

Faith lives in conscience alone. And when we turn lovingly to the testimonies of our past, then this knowledge has only a passively supporting effect, not actively supporting.

Conscience is there to shape attitude, not to look for end end to our search.

Whoever asks for one final piece of truth in the world (such as an ultimately meaning of life) has not found that cause in God. Even the scientist denies this vain and desirable question, if he holds faith. Because the spirit can only recognize the cause or reason of things alone, but never the primordial origination itself. The spirit must be able to grow beyond itself.

God is the primal thing of experience. Namely he is within everything, since everything is embraced by him.

Conscience is the primordial part of faith, decision in God. Judgment of the inner nature, the moral of man.

The spirit is the primordial part of consciousness. Decision in God. Judgment on the external nature of the human world.

Mind is the primary part of consciousness. Decision in God. Judgment on the external nature of the human world.

The intangible and unattainable always extends beyond the tangible, yet remains part of it, the conscience must always grasp knowledge. Otherwise without this spark of conscience, knowledge becomes directionless, lifeless, dead.

Knowledge and conscience, knowledge and faith do not complement each other, but reside within each other. Where there is no consciousness there can be no conscience, and where there is no conscience, there is no right consciousness, no right knowledge.

So what is faith?
The primal part of personal life. Determined by experience, determining for life.

So what is God?
The original thing in personal life. Determination of experience, determination of life.

God is reality restraint to experience and world-wide effect within the souls of men, not world-wide reality (Nazarene) and experience-based intervention (revelation, miracle).

Uncertainty in the deepest, striving for security, is natural to faith. Uncertainty, but in the great basic insights and intentions of the species, comes only from the millennia-long mutilation of the German soul, of the German conscience. From its suppression in its nature and compulsive obedience in its language. Through centuries of needless inanimation and inadequate energy to spring. That must be overcome now, and for the future.

The only reason that a people like the German could become alien in their beliefs, was that they were alienated in their politics and worldview. Because where a people has become a stranger to their path and plan, the faith in the species is without a visible vow, a visible effect, and can be replaced in the visible by another belief, which mutilates in reaching back into the unseen, the soul.

And the people can be alienated because the belief was instilled from above by a foreign political leadership (Chlodwig, Karl der Franke, etc.) and from below through an foreign spiritual leadership (Ulfilas, Bonifatius, etc.) in the whole public life. Life was cut off; decisive only through the political will from above, because those not taken from their own beliefs were few among the Nordic peoples below.

Politically, the alien faith gained more power than a single people that had ancestral roots, thence hidden from them. These foreign beliefs were a tool, deriving power over souls, they became secured in more than one people across this earth.

And so it went until the day that the people thought about themselves, and wanted to gain and own themselves and their destiny again. Then the path and the plan were sought again out of conscience, out of the certainties of the species, and in this their faith came to life again.

Christianity seemed to live in three basic doctrines for the Germans, to live indispensably in the pressure of the historical proof of God, but in this way it was not openly oppression of a culture: the just God and loving father stood for the necessity in destiny and healing omnipotence of the Nature, compassion for the national duty and eternal life in the hereafter, for the eternity of life par excellence. This was how Christianity was Germanized until its justice, love and immortality also became questionable, until Germanism became so powerful that it could be Christianized no longer.

Where is the "positive" aspect of German belief in God?

In God. And through God in the German people. And through the German conscience committed to God in the reality that Germany faces.

Do not ask what the written laws of German belief in God are. If you ask in this way, you haven't found yourself in them. Because the laws of German faith are not written, but inscribed in your blood. Courage, honor, loyalty, these basic virtues of all proficient races, have their particular color and liveliness in faith and are stated implicitly, or not.

It is the positive German belief in God that something unspeakable, which you call God nonetheless, urges you in your soul to maintain these codes of honor, to make them visible in the world of your designs by fulfilling the necessities of your being.

The positive German belief in God lies in the fact that God creates something positive in the world; in God through people.

The success of these efforts is not an expression of divine election based on the Calvinist model. Rather, it is strict loyalty to species, relentless self-succession are signs of the divine fate within us. That will finally prove to be a success. Because the lovingly, spiritually, and mentally healthy man is right. He is fulfilled in striving, and less-so, the strivingless, happiness.

Something in our life pushes us to believe. And this faith urges us, in its completion compels us to allow some insight and intent within us, to let inner and outer reality manifest inside of us. In this life we act, we impress upon life the same way it does upon us.

Insight comes from life and is at the same time intention in the faith, which also comes from life.

Why shouldn't the "positive" be within us, since it should come from ourselves? If it came from elsewhere, we would still be there! And living would still turn out to be worthy! Then was all this personal effort worthwhile?

We have not and need not creeds, save for those that can and implore to take action. Deed is our creed and confession. Deed alone.

We seek knowledge in faith and confession in life. Life experience and life decision are the means to do this.

In the open, healthy sense, reality has an inner statement of how life has to be shaped, in order to find one's way in oneself, in order to align with oneself.

It is only necessary to insert yourself into the entirety. That alone is morality. In the entirety of one's own soul, of one people's soul and the world soul, which we ourselves are in three circles of experience. A wrong path is always something in the middle of two halves, not the whole.

Basically one seeks an inner self-establishment and accommodation. Not an external one, as has become the basic principle of many people, people who have sacrificed their souls to the god of the stomach, of the lustful body.

Here, faith is a necessity. Morality is necessity itself.

Life, within itself, always rescues poverty. And what turns over hardship can only be moral. Turned over inwardly. First and last, initially and finally. The deed exists only in between this.

Our hardship is a burden to us. Inner poverty puts us under pressure. The greatest hardship and the greatest happiness of men is to destroy both.

In us, hardship becomes necessity.

Why a man is more pushed out of God than another and has more energy available in that drive, depends only on his race. The power to rear up and overcome from shallows, the laws we don't even suspect; but which include race and kind. Because race and kind, are ultimately infinite, like all living things.

There is no good nor evil, at least as they are understood by the petty tributes demanded of the Christian God, but only strength or insufficiency, power and powerlessness. Like everything in life, depending on the type and the hour.

The aim of strength is so weakness is discovered, and turned into strength. And weakness, between need and necessity, that is the tension that is inherent in German belief in God. In its transformation, strength is only preserved and increased. Weakness is untapped strength, strength is defeated weakness. This struggle between strength and weakness, between hardship and necessity, this is the inner tension of the German belief in God.

In this struggle it is good to be, or to become, quite sure of the basic certainties of one's belief in life's many facets. Our deep German language, in which the word renders the meaning complete - we have to listen to the word carefully for its meaning.

From Destiny.

Destiny is what emerges from us, not what approaches us. We have to accept it. Not suffer because of it.

Destiny means salvation. Destiny is a healing, holy, and salvation bringing life within us. Life that we have mastered and therefore have preserved within us.

Providence, that which is foreseen by God, that which is foreseen by the priests, that is Christianity. The Germans use this word also for favorable good fate (*geschick*).[1] Destiny (*schicksal*) that became the finest, threatening, violent, overwhelming.

How something emerges from a man depends on his inner self. Through his basic insights and basic intentions of life.

Destiny is a pure inner necessity. Life gives us opportunities which, through our grasped inner-self, become apparent external necessities. But the opportunity through us is only opportunity and otherwise invisible, dead.

---

[1] In the original translation, the English word identified with these passages was fate. However the editor posits from Bartsch's descriptions that fate is not the key word here, but destiny, as—

"*Fate is not synonymous with destiny, but the opposite to it. Fate attributes necessity to the incidents of a life, but destiny is the inner necessity of the organism. An incident can wipe out a life, and thus terminate its destiny, but this event came from outside the organism, and thus* [while fate] *was apart from its destiny.*" - Francis Parker Yockey, in <u>Imperium</u>

The destiny of an acorn, apart from causality-thinking and rational dissection of *how* it becomes a tree, is to grow into an oak, and produce as many branches and future acorns as it may. The fate of that tree, be it to the axe or the storm, is something apart from this.

Life is not destiny, the species is.

Life is only a call to attitude, since it wants to be ready for its kind of destiny.

Knowledge of destiny always gives security or uncertainty, depending on whether the certainties of the species were able to give security or not. There is rest in restlessness, or restlessness in renunciation, as life requires it.

The Nordic man, in particular, has a deep unruly peace, restless, which has been turned into a sinfulness by the ingenious priestly spirit, through the naiveté of our ancestors. But this is a combative loss of peace which has drawn forth the greatest achievements of the world.

Germanic people are contemplative, often subtle and deep. That is why the other peoples sit like frightened fowl around Germany's borders. You never know what can suddenly erupt from this strange German people.

German people know about the hardship and darkness that life has also. One often has a lot to carry in life. But bears it well. Not in a renunciation or shortsighted rebellion, but in a creative sense.

Life can only be overcome with life. With new, greater vitality.

Life has its meaning in destiny. Life comes to us in an unshaped way and is shaped through us. Any other meaning that one attaches to life does not fulfill it.

The question of the meaning of life in the world will always be futile. The world simply does not answer.

We must answer. We must find the answer in ourselves. We have to set, realize the meaning that we want to see as content of the world. It will only have meaning when we have granted it our meaning.

Whoever thinks fate is not an act of divine providence doesn't need to be meaningless, purposeless, cruel.

The old peoples didn't think this way. This is Christian thinking as well. When externally considered, nature is nothing, when nature must maintain itself, then it must be "meaningless", "purposeless", and "cruel" as well.

Meaning and purpose are small elements of a larger context. So are our personal lives within the comprehensive existence. But they are not existence itself.

Let us see the necessity behind the "cruelty". As life is set up this way, it must be "cruel" to exist in itself. In particular, also the needless would be meaningless and purposeless.

All of this is Christian resentment carried in nature, in original sin. Renunciation of life, and mercy, which are one and the same, are born of Christianity. Only nonsense not in the unnatural aspect of the hidden sense.

We should not be relinquishing and merciful where life is concerned, but insatiable and relentless.

The living man, who creates in unity with nature, knows only the peace and tranquility of the night.

From Guilt.

It is not a matter of preventing sins by renouncing life and erasing them by the mercy of forgiveness. Rather the eternal guilt for life, of our life and entire existence, is not a fault, but a duty, that must be felt and redeemed.

The divine light which shines in us and becomes the shadow of insights and intentions within us, is only apparent because there is also a darkness inside of us. We only see the darkness because light lives within.
Even in the brightest deed, a shadow remains within life, even as this is not all of life. Because man cannot erase this aspect of himself in action.

The shadow is not a crown of thorns on the head of man. It can be the crown of a king, when there is a sign of the light also dwells within us.

Horror seizes our hearts as when Germanic fates (wyrds) were issued in old tales and legends. But nowhere else is the luminosity of the soul as strong.

That is why the German is not a man of opposites. Light and shadow are opposites only to the eye. He is human in a completely comprehensive sense: human of all heights and depths. That is why he is a creator of great history and culture.

All life is naturally innocent, in a moral sense. But not without duty in morality, and in the political.

Guilt does not indicate deficiencies that are depressing, but a deficiency that needs to be remedied. It was priestly work to twist this political sense of guilt against the Germans, into the moral sense of sin.

Guilt can be difficult, it can make you deeply unhappy. But it also has a freeing, combative meaning in itself.

The Commitment of the Will.

There can only be sin where there is, and should be, free will. Because what the man does and must do, without any reason coming from its own nature, is to sin.

Without free will there wouldn't be any original sin, and it wouldn't require any mercy. How enterprising of the old Jewish God Jehovah to instill this mechanism in humans. The man and goods will always have to return to him, who has all the rights for their preparation and also for their repair. The only bad thing is that he let so much spirit grow in men, that the goods could ask themselves, whether the manufacturer couldn't have worked better and where he got the audacity to consider them responsible for their own mistakes.

Where life prepares its fate, where racial laws apply, there can be no free will. Even behind the indecisiveness and second-thought, which can precede a decision, there is a full being, nothing but a certain being of man. And the same behind the decision itself.

The people's will is linked to its species. It comes from the species, it is linked to the being.

The species is free in its will. At least it can be. Because species all have purposes in themselves.

We say: Our will is species-bound, our right will is free.

Free will is clear air in sin.
Lack of responsibility from men is the last judgment to God.

Will to be, that is responsibility and liberation of men.

From the Eternal.

The beginning and end of life are only the passage points of existence in a human being, where they get lost in an afterlife, they also mean life responsibility.

Only in life itself stems eternity. Man is a rising and setting figure within it. In the same way the sea makes itself clear in one wave among others on the horizon, but takes it back, that it may appear in millions of others.

Man only has a part in the eternity of life as long as he lives. Not after he has lived. This is again the profound, serious and liberating, active meaning of the Germanic certainty of life.

Only as long as man lives is he also eternal. Only as long as his blood lives on in a living man. Birth is not the beginning of sin, and death is not its end of judgment.

But birth is direction and death is direction. Let us make sure that we have reached death. With us.

Where death has not liberated, it is not a point behind the last breath expressed in sentences, it cannot be experienced, and loved as a godfather and friend, Death. Death, a friend who takes great fatigue out of life- if your breath breaks off roughly or does not even appear to be there, it should not make life appear questionable and bitter, but rather direct you to the unquestionable, the great riddle of life, and make you silent in it.

Man only desires when he has no answer. And the answer to death is life. The meaningful life.

No striving can be without intellectual, spiritual or physical need. Death is life too. An event of life. We want to be touched only by death when we are old. But the woeful dashing of a young life also speaks of the brazen, liberating law of necessity.

Coincidence is only the outward appearance of an event; its inner is always necessity, since it has grasped people.

Divine "providence" and the "coincidence" of life are, in reality without forgiveness, against God and life. Both are eternally accounted for by man and throughout a man's life, this bill is unpaid. Men make God and life their debtors, and in doing so men deceive both.

And do not seek consolation and liberation in God from reflection alone, but in the act of loving among one another. Love is a gift from the soul; it cannot be given commands. Duty rises in you and grants you consolation and liberation. Be necessary to each other. In God.

Be called from the death of another, to still more deeply immerse yourself in the laws of life. And by doing so you will have made this death fruitful, stripped it of its bitterness.

Life goes through you, is inside of you. It does not become more than you give, it does not diminish when it takes you. It only seems for a moment to be limited in terms of its shape, but not in terms of its shaping power.

You yourself are not a real beginning, or a real end. You are part of eternity in God, when you have lived God. Because God's eternity grows in all experience.

Be German men, this is your belief! See, this is it! How could you have resisted it?

Make it alive in yourself in its complete essence!

As long as Christianity was the religion in Germany, which was not a religion by or of your people, there were non-believers among you. Who found themselves to be unbelieving because they were too strong-hearted against this foreign belief, which in bitterest of hard times could not and did not want to change bitter hardship.

There the faith arose in you, which you call the new, despite it being as old and as inherent as your blood essence. This is what you must know and recognize, confess to yourself.

It is not important that you are no longer be part of the community of Christians, but it is paramount to learn to laugh at the shame of endless existential sin and guilt, and only feel such guilt, bound in the duty that you must commit to the wellbeing your people. The true exit from that belief system is a consequence of this conviction alone.

Because the feeling of sin is truly the root of Christianity.

The priest caste can say against all doubts: infinite wisdom! Against all despair: infinite goodness, infinite love! Infinite wisdom, infinite goodness, infinite love, that are so great that you can not understand them. That is why they come from God.

The real attitude to life alone cannot be refuted and distorted.

Therefore live in your day and your eternity paganly. That means lives without artificial restriction because those natural laws stem from the law of your kind, your species, your people.

Let life swell in yourself: fresh, cheerful, bubbling, threatening, violent, dark and clear. How it is and the way that it becomes necessary.

Be immortal in God through your faith! Be the salt of the earth and harvesting in your fertility!
Know this: a belief is worth as much as it is able to naturally foster life without forcing it.

It is in the decisive difficulty of the German situation that the people must recognize, that their essence has always lived in this belief, only lives through this belief. That this belief is also a faith. That this faith must arise in common consciousness, against the grip of Christianity, before it has complete and open rights in our land. Before the people of our kind can become aware and conscious of it. They can then fulfill and be fulfilled.

The events of our day have the strongest effect thereon; to take it to the deepest means to come to God in the growing German belief in God— but it also requires a movement in which the believers already have reliable and firm representation in their beliefs.

It is the decisive difficulty of this movement, which is the innermost of its political aspect, which also drives and lives in it, that it travels in its mission to the people. Its mission in the way in which God is alive to the people who want to live in God.

Uncertainties and insecurities are the whole issue of the German belief in God. Both may only be redeemed in a soul of conviction. To grasp them, first and foremost, is the gift and task of these movements.

Morality is a decision within men. Political decision is between them. Faith bears both. And has effects on both of these concepts. It has to do firstly and lastly with living, breathing, men, in which all decisions are made.

Only when this is understood will German belief in God spread like fire, jump from man to man among the people, and the flame of life will be revealed to serve us all.

The positive aspect of life is faith.

The positive aspect of faith is God.

The positive God is life.

The God-Believers' Catechism

Originally Issued by Der Reichsring der Gottgläubigen Deutschen

1. *Why do we call ourselves Believers in God?*
   We call ourselves believers in God because we believe with all the depths of our soul as did our ancestors, in the Divinity.

2. *What is the Divinity?*
   We reject every anthropomorphic characteristic of God implied in such phrases as: a jealous God, God the avenger, anger of God. The word of God and the personal inspiration of the prophets by God are things extraneous to the faith; hidden revelations belong to the realm of pious legends.

3. *How do we know there is a Divinity?*
   (*a*) From the existence of our people. While the individual is born and dies, the people remains. The people is eternal according to human judgment. Its eternity is derived from its blood. In the blood of the people is contained the mysterious force from which new life continually develops. This force that gives Life is the Divinity.
   (*b*) From the existence of nature and the order of life. The ordered change in the Seasons, the fixed courses of the stars, high and low tides, the regular succession of day and night testify in forcible manner to the work of that same eternal force which we discover in the coursing of our blood, in the birth and death of beings.

4. *Is there a Science of God?*
No: God or The Divinity are too infinite to be the object of scientific research, too incomprehensible to be explained by human conceptions.

5. *What are the relations of Man with The Divinity?*
Man feels acutely that he has within him a divine law of life. He becomes conscious of the fact: God lives in us. He stands awed before the conviction that the eternal divine force is at work within him. Not fear of God, but regard for his own dignity and duty, characterizes his experience of God.

6. *What duties devolve unto Man as a result of his experience of God?*
Purity and the care of the body; increased bodily strength. Sport controlled for the service of the Divine in Man. Perfecting of all the spiritual forces, intelligence, will, sensibility. The care and protection of human society, the family, kindred, the people, because in the apogee of human society, the Divine grows even more manifest.

7. *Is there a Moral Law for Man?*
Yes, it is twofold. The unwritten one in our blood and the written one of human society. The unwritten moral law is the voice of our blood, our memory, and the blood being the seat of the divine source of life, the voice is a divine voice. (Natural law.) The written social law has grown out of ancient customs. The law of a nation is the written law arising from the moral exigencies of our blood, of our race.

8. *What interior support has Man?*
Inborn and modified by race— honor. From the conviction that we have written within us the divine law comes that strong sense of honor that is for man both a bond and a warning. Society: in the notion of Society (family, the people) are strong moral ties, some visible, others hidden. Injuries to Society always involve injuries to the individual.

9. *What is the purpose of Man's life?*

Man lives to fulfill the law of his life. And that is the transmission of life (the Man lives for his Son) and the service of the people, the most important source of the law of life. By so doing one may fulfill the mission of one's life; the manner in which it is done is not important. The life of a man in which these two duties are avoided has no meaning.

10. *In what does the religious life of Believers consist?*

Above all in the completion of an active life of the divine mission in us. Man bowing in veneration and calm recognition before the divine mystery, concentrating on the divine law within us which also gives a deep meaning to solemn hours. Special feasts are, the birth of a child, the giving of its name, the death of a man, funeral rites; the entry of youths into adolescence, the dedication or consecration of youth; in the alteration of the position of the sun, Solstice; in the breaking of spring—Easter—May; the harvest of Autumn—October, and the Yule ceremonies of December.

11. *Is there an eternity?*

Eternity concerns our land and our people, and both find expression in one concept. In our land are laid to rest our forefathers, and one day our grandchildren will also rest there; the people, however, carry on into the future their actions, as their heritage is intact. Without this earth and this people, eternity would not exist as we know it. We know not a greater immortality than man's deeds, how we manifest in God thereafter is beyond our comprehension. Therefore we speak of an Eternal nation.

12. *What are the relations between a God "believer" and Christianity?*

He has a religious belief, and has no need of that of other peoples. For him the revelation offered by nature and the people, the duties that devote upon him from his blood, and the conviction that he survives in his people, is enough. Christianity can offer to the believer in God nothing that can give him greater faith and conviction, a stronger force, and a firmer foundation.

13. *Who can legitimately call himself a Believer in God?*

A Believer in God is he who has returned to his distinctive beliefs and has freed himself from every foreign tie. He breaks these by deferring to competent authority of his own people, and declaring his exit from the Church because he does not recognize any other tie than that which binds him to them.

14. *How can the Believer in God help his people?*

He can enroll himself in the "fronte volontaire" of the voluntary combatants for a German belief in God, who are organized in a sworn body of comrades in the national circle of German Believers in God (*Reichsring der Gottglaubigen Deutschen*). The purpose of this organization is to help in uniting the people in faith.

A NOTE FROM THE EDITOR

The preceding pages represent two different treatises, one long-form missive and another condensed catechism. The former, by Dr. Heinz Bartsch, represents a treatise on matters of the mindset of god-belief, those who have chosen to believe in God despite having found no confidence in Christian doctrine. The latter was issued by the National Ring of German God-believers (*Reichsring der Gottglaubigen Deutschen*), and covers many of the same topics in brief as questions and answers.

These writings were a response to Kirchenkampf, as the clergy came at odds with the government and supporters of National Socialist Germany. Nevertheless atheism was regarded as synonymous with hubris and degeneracy, or the factions of the Communists to the East. Although only a small fraction of Germans identified as *gottgläubig* in a census of the time, the message of these groups was broadcast by the RRG, state radio.

The notion that this religion of the Second World War was a new creation, is only partially true. Today we know from scholarly research that pre-Christian European and Vedic scripture did indeed refer to a God above the pantheons many refer to in mythology, a sky-father known by different names, most prominently as Dyeus Pater.

www.ingramcontent.com/pod-product-compliance
Lightning Source LLC
Chambersburg PA
CBHW030311100526
44590CB00012B/599